Continuity of Government

Ronald N. Goulden, MBA, PMP

Continuity of Government

Copyright © 2016

Ronald N. Goulden, MBA, PMP

ALL RIGHTS RESERVED

Cover design by Ronald Goulden

ISBN: 978-1533118349

Table of Contents

Introduction

In a world of ever-increasing uncertainty and fear, we all look for some stability in our lives. Everywhere we look, we see crime and famine and war that increases every day.

Our governments seem powerless or unwilling to stop this carnage. Rather than acting like petulant children, we need the governments of the world to act responsibly and protect their citizens and honor the social contract they have with the people.

In order to accomplish this function, it may be necessary for the government to take reasonable steps to ensure that it can still effectively function on behalf of the citizenry.

Continuity of Government (CoG), is just that, the act of providing the governments of the world with the ability to continue to function in the event of an emergency.

That is a lofty and noble-sounding description. At first blush, it makes sense. After all, in the event of a tremendous crisis, the governments of the world must be able to continue to function and rally resources to solve the emergency, right?

However, what could initiate a Continuity of Government event reminds me of a time when I attended a meeting hosted by a private equity firm that was acquiring my employer.

The spokesman stood proudly on the stage with the business leaders behind him. He waved his arm expansively behind him to indicate the business leaders and said, "My Company is buying yours because it has been grossly mismanaged by the people sharing this stage with me."

He talked for a few minutes then waved his arm to again include the managers he had so recently accused of ruining the business and proudly proclaimed, "These are the people who have proven they can effectively manage your company, they will stay on to rebuild the company; the rest of you can clean out your desks and go home, we have no more need for you."

Like the inept managers in this example, if our world leaders make such a mess of things that they have to invoke CoG, who do you think will be saved? Certainly not the common man who paid for all of the technology, intelligence gathering, and construction of the bunkers that the elites will cower in while the world is destroyed.

It seems that the people who create and foster these world-changing events that could evoke a Continuity of Government type of action are the very people who will use CoG as a shield to hide behind, on the pretext of 'fixing the problem'.

I have to ask if we want the people who caused so much damage that the logical solution is for them to hide and protect themselves in a bunker, to try to take charge and correct the problems they create? That's kind of like expecting the arsonist to put out the fires he started. Somehow, that logic just doesn't seem logical.

You can rest assured that our 'leaders', the world elites, will dash to the safety of their bunkers and hide while humanity withers. Their solution to any serious crisis will be to protect themselves at your expense.

By definition, CoG will only protect the important 'leaders'.

Think about that for a moment. Only those deemed 'important' will be protected. And just who gets to make that decision? The very people who caused the problem.

When a national disaster is declared, will you and your family be invited into the safety of a hardened bunker? No, and any attempt to force your way in will invoke a lethal response.

When the government apparently fails, will they protect your from looters and rapists? No.

Will the government, from the safety of its bunker, provide you with fresh food, water, and medical aid? No.

Have you seen ANY of the plans for Continuity of Government? Have you received instructions about what to do in the event of a critical emergency? Do you know where the nearest safe haven is located or even if you will be permitted to enter it?

The answer to all of these questions is, NO. The very people who are supposed to protect and defend the citizens, (you and your family) have acted in secret for decades building survival bunkers for their preservation so that your family can die, very likely in extreme agony and horror. Why should such an entity be allowed to survive and perpetuate itself?

What is the government likely to do while working under the auspices of CoG?

If it does anything, it will most likely enact some form of Martial Law and invoke any or all of the following Executive Orders, in which, among other things, the government has granted itself the right to force you and your family into FEMA 'concentration' camps and disperse you and your family to forced labor sites at their discretion, you may never see your family again.

Keep in mind that Executive Orders (EO) are, by definition, official documents, numbered consecutively, through which the President of the United States manages the operations of the Federal Government.

That is to say that Presidents may issue Executive Orders to help officers and agencies of the executive branch manage the operations within the federal government itself.

Executive orders have the full force of law, since issuances are typically made in pursuance of certain Acts of Congress, some of which specifically delegate to the President some degree of discretionary power or are believed to take authority from a power granted directly to the Executive by the Constitution.

However, Executive Orders were NEVER intended to circumvent the Legislative process or to strip citizens of their fundamental rights.

- **EXECUTIVE ORDER 10990** – {Transportation} - gives the government control over all modes of transportation and highways and seaports. (This means they take your car from you for their discretionary use. Even bicycles may be confiscated.)
- **EXECUTIVE ORDER 10995**– {Communications} - gives the government the authority to seize and control the entirety of the communication network. (Guess what happens to that expensive phone you just bought…it will be in the sweaty palm of some petty bureaucrat.)
- **EXECUTIVE ORDER 10997** – {Power & Fuel} - enables the government to take over all electrical power, gas, petroleum, fuels and minerals. (Including the fuel in your car's gas tank and your lawn mower.)
- **EXECUTIVE ORDER 10998** – {Food} - grants the government the power to take over ALL food resources and farms. (This includes the food in your kitchen cabinets and your garden.)
- **EXECUTIVE ORDER 11000** – {Labor} - permits the government to mobilize civilians into work brigades under government supervision; families can be separated. (Forced labor and the division of families to further control the masses.)

- **EXECUTIVE ORDER 11001** – {Health} - gives the government control over all health, education and welfare functions. (All medicines now belong to the government, to be allocated as they see fit. All of those life-sustaining medications that you have to take regularly can be confiscated by any petty bureaucrat.)
- **EXECUTIVE ORDER 11002** – {The List} - designates that the Postmaster General is to manage a national registration of all persons. (I can't imagine why they would want a list of everyone?)
- **EXECUTIVE ORDER 11003** – {Aircraft} - allows the government to take over all airports and aircraft, including commercial aircraft. (No more air travel; and if you own an aircraft, it now belongs to the government. This might be a good thing if it results in the dismantling of TSA.)
- **EXECUTIVE ORDER 11004** – {Housing} - grants the Housing and Finance Authority the power to relocate communities, build new housing with public funds, designate areas to be abandoned, and establish new locations for populations. (They can force you to house others or take your house from you entirely.)
- **EXECUTIVE ORDER 11005** – {Shipping & Transport} - enables the government to assume control of railroads, streets and roads, inland waterways and public storage facilities. (Your stocked ponds and lakes, and the contents of your personal storage locker will belong to the government.)
- **EXECUTIVE ORDER 11051** – {FEMA in Charge} - designates the responsibility of the Office of Emergency Planning and grants authorization to activate all Executive Orders in times of increased international tensions and economic or financial crisis. (FEMA will become the supreme ruler of the country…making and enforcing laws as deemed necessary. The interesting thing about this is that only the Director of FEMA can determine when things are normalized enough to return control to the elected government.)
- **EXECUTIVE ORDER 11310** – {Legal} - gives authority to the Department of Justice to enforce the Executive Orders, to institute industrial support, to establish judicial and legislative liaison, to control all aliens, to operate penal and correctional institutions, and to advise and assist the

President. (The Constitution and Bill of Rights no longer exist. Anything the President or Director of FEMA writes as an Executive Order, now becomes the 'law of the land'.)

- **EXECUTIVE ORDER 11049** – {EO Consolidation} - assigns emergency preparedness function to federal departments and agencies, and consolidates 21 operative Executive Orders issued over a fifteen year period. (Executive Orders never die, they just get updated and renamed. This is a back-up in case someone pushed hard enough to rescind an EO…the onerous mandates just live on in some other EO.)

- **EXECUTIVE ORDER 11921** – {Production} - demands that the Federal Emergency Preparedness Agency establish control of production and distribution, energy sources, wages, salaries, credit and the flow of money in U.S. and financial institution in any undefined national emergency. It also stipulates that when a state of emergency is declared by the President, Congress cannot review the action for six months. (You no longer have to worry about earning a living…your efforts belong to the government.) By the way, this EO makes Congress and the Supreme Court obsolete. (I'll bet the nimrods in Congress do not realize this.)

I will go into greater detail about the more Onerous Executive Orders in an upcoming publication.

Now, as you research the Executive Orders, you will find that many of the Executive Orders listed above may be designated as 'rescinded' or 'repealed'. However, that is just a smokescreen.

If these orders are 'rescinded', rest assured that they are embodied in subsequent Executive Orders. The government will never willingly relinquish any power or authority it has granted itself.

Under CoG, you can expect door to door raiding by government personnel and petty bureaucrats, taking everything that might be of value, (EO 10998) while advising you to report to your nearest FEMA site (EO 11000). (They may even burn your house to force you to go to the FEMA camp.)

Throughout the verbiage of the Executive Orders, one sees reference to the Government and its agents or designees.

Just who is the government at this point? Practically anyone with a position to assert influence over you and yours.

There may be a lot of false confiscations and abductions as predators seize on this rich opportunity. (How can you tell if an official is really official and acting within the limits of his or her power?)

Always remember that CoG is just for the protection of our elite 'leaders'. Everyone else is expendable.

Of course, Americans will scream about the Constitution and the Bill of Rights. However, with the Executive Orders, the government has conveniently provided itself with a mechanism to suspend the Constitution and all rights of the citizenry.

Remember that during a declared 'State of Emergency' the citizens become property, to be disposed of at the whim of whatever petty bureaucrat has been granted control over your life. (Always keep in mind that in the eyes of most 'elites', the common man and woman are the most worthless of commodities, and readily expendable.)

Weapons will be collected with extreme prejudice. (In my mind's eye, I see the government forces showing up at a house with a platoon of infantry and a tank. They may ask for all weapons and if there is any hesitation or resistance, the tank simply destroys the house and anything inside and then moves on to the next house.)

There would be no option for a 'stand-off' to wait for re-enforcements; they will take what they want and move on. Pray that all they want is your weapons and not your wives, sisters, and daughters. ("They have the might therefore, right or wrong, they're always right".)

During a 'State of Emergency' expect the manifestation of a very 'heavy-handed' government presence.

When you hear the phrase, "Continuity of Government", be afraid, not proud or comforted.

Where did CoG Start?

The British Government is credited with developing the modern concept of Continuity of Government just before and during World War II in response to the threat of German Luftwaffe bombing.

However, paranoid rulers have planned for Continuity of Government since the beginning of time, they just did not give it the snazzy name.

European castles are merely fortresses for the Royals to hide in during bad times, leaving the commoners and peasants outside to deal with whatever terror inspired the Royals to hide from the threat, whether it was Viking hordes or the plague.

Ancient rulers in Egypt, Babylonia, Greece, Rome, as well as in the Medieval, and Renaissance times all built majestic palaces, castles, and fortresses with the labor of slaves and peasants.

While these magnificent structures were seemingly testaments to the power and majesty of the nation, their real purpose was to protect the Royals. The commoners realized no direct benefits from these majestic edifices.

In theory, the common people could seek sanctuary in these structures during time of war or danger. In reality, most commoners were turned away. Every meal a commoner ate was one less meal for the Royals. (Remember, the idea is to preserve the 'elites' at the expense of the commoners.)

History speaks of the wonders of the ancient civilizations without discussing how those wonders were built, and how many people died so that the 'Royals' would have a magnificent palace to reside in while the citizens lived in disease and squalor.

Was the work performed by willing contractors or by expendable slaves and conscripted laborers? That is a foolish question, not worthy of an answer. The wonders of the world were built by the blood and lives of millions, to glorify a few wealthy 'leaders'.

There can be no question that the ancient 'Royals' believed in Continuity of Government as much as their twenty-first Century descendants.

Throughout history, the money and efforts of the common citizens have been confiscated to build edifices to protect the Royals ('leaders', 'elites', the rich and famous).

No 'elite', 'royal', or 'leader' built anything with their own hands or with their own funds; they took from others to glorify themselves, and they will do anything to retain that glory. THAT is Continuity of Government. It has nothing to do with government, but everything to do with power.

It is a flaw in human nature to allow 'leaders' to dominate and control the masses for their own benefit, at the expense of the masses. Historically, the 'leaders' always received special treatment, portions, and protection, while the everyday citizen suffered.

I have witnessed on numerous occasional where a 'famous' or 'wealthy' person would be escorted to the head of the line in public venues, passing those who may have been waiting for hours.

I have seen the father of a very poor household, buy a basketball multi-millionaire a drink or offer to pay for his meal.

Under no circumstances did I see the 'rich and famous' reject or decline these offerings, or give anything in return except a smile and maybe a 'Thanks' or a signature scrawled on a napkin.

The concept of 'Continuity of Government' or the Darwinian 'Survival of the Fittest', is a common theme in nature.

In most 'social' species, there is typically a dominant male or female that enjoys the privilege of feeding first and being able to pick the most desirable mates.

Watch a pride of lions or a pack of wolves. The leader is treated with deference and only rarely challenged. When the leader has sated its hunger, then the lesser members may feed.

You can even observe this with your household dog. The canine may sit and drool and lick its lips as you eat; this is because it recognizes you as the 'Alpha' and is waiting for its turn to eat; it expects you to share the leftovers with it.

At the human level, Continuity of Government actually stems from mankind's innate and flawed willingness to elevate others above themselves, sacrificing their rights and dignity to the benefit of others. Throughout history the 'leaders' have capitalized on this human flaw.

Look through history; in every epoch and every culture, there have always been the 'haves' and the rest of the world. In many instances, the 'leaders' have self-proclaimed that they were appointed by whatever god is relevant for the culture to rule the masses, and to live their lives of luxury at the expense of the common citizen. No one has ever questioned this divine assignment.

The funny thing about these self-anointed 'leaders' is that they have no real qualifications to lead, other than possessing a bit more aggressiveness than the rest of the human herd.

These individuals speak out vociferously, or beat down those that might be a threat, and suddenly, they become trusted 'leaders', endowed with magnificent knowledge and wisdom.

The CoG mentality is not reserved for politicians alone. Virtually any organized human activity utilizes a form of CoG to ensure that the 'leader' is well-taken care of.

Churches continually grow, asking or demanding tithes from the members. Jesus taught on hilltops under the sky, why do modern pastors and priests require multi-million dollar churches and luxury automobiles and aircraft? The answer is that the people willingly empower these parasites to leech their livelihood from others.

There is a dearth of humble leaders in the history of humanity. Most leaders are merciless, unless it serves their purpose to be otherwise. They act decisively and swiftly before others can bolster a defense or raise an argument, thus seizing the reins of power.

Most politicians today have been hand-picked and follow the mandates of their party and the real 'leaders'. There is no sitting politician that will place the citizens or even the government above their own greedy desires.

They will do everything possible to ensure the continuance of their current life of power and privilege and constantly seek greater power.

Rest assured that your Congress man or woman, your elected official, is well aware of the CoG bunkers and is trying to do everything possible to be included, if they aren't already.

Ask your Representative or Senator about CoG and they will recite the party line for you, but will dance away from more detailed questions, such as: "What specific threats do you anticipate? How many of your constituents will be granted access to the bunkers?"

This travesty will perpetuate until such time as the citizens drag their 'leaders' from their sanctuaries and force them to stand with the rest of the citizenry. Until that time, the 'leaders' of the world feel they have no accountability to or responsibility for the citizens.

Why CoG?

Why do we need Continuity of Government? As I said, on the surface, planning for Continuity of Government sounds like a good thing to do. After all, the primary mission of the government is to protect its citizens, and that cannot happen if the Government is at risk.

In times of war, the 'leaders' should be able to protect themselves from external dangers so that they can continue to manage the country and look after the best interests and survival of the people.

When you have a benign government, led by people who place the country above their personal greed, then Continuity of Government planning and the corresponding activities are good.

However, no 'leader' selflessly places his or her country before themselves. "Leaders' of modern countries and even the more barbaric countries are most concerned with their own self-interests. They tend to be out of touch with humanity and their citizens.

If a 'leader' or government values itself above its citizens, than that government should be abolished because it is not serving the needs of the people. The self-serving 'leaders' should be dragged into the courtyard and immediately tried and executed for treason. At the very least, the 'leaders' have violated the implied social contract they have with their citizens.

In the past, during the pre-nuclear age, the Concept of Continuity of Government had some validity.

When the most extreme form of aggression was conventional bombing, it was a reasonable option for the leadership to retreat to underground bunkers until the bombers passed. The actual damage could be localized. Typically, there was ample advanced warning of the attack.

Today, with the proliferation of chemical, biological, and nuclear weaponry, a major attack will result in a decimated populace and crippled countries.

With no citizens remaining and virtually no viable enemies (a nuclear or biological war will essentially destroy all life and permanently alter the geo-political alignment of the world forever), the concept of Continuity of Government becomes exposed for what it really is.

CoG is a plan designed to protect and preserve the lives and lifestyles of the elites of the world. It has nothing to do with Continuity of Government and protecting the country or its citizens.

If there is only one spot left in the bunker, and if you, as the last mechanic in the world, are competing against a billionaire for that spot, who do you honestly think will be brought into the bunker? (Let me give you a hint; it won't be you.) The elites will protect theirs and defend their station in life above all others.

Any 'commoners' who might be selected for preservation will be 'saved' for labor or 'entertainment'.

Trigger Events

What could possibly trigger a CoG action plan? The short and correct answer is simply, 'anything'.

If an event occurs that makes enough of our 'leaders' nervous, they will declare a CoG event and implement some variant of Martial Law, suspend the Constitution, send Congress and the Supreme Court home, and dismiss all of the bureaucrats, or just let them die at their posts.

Obviously, an attack by a hostile nation would be a trigger event, and might possibly even be justifiable. However, **just the fear of a hostile attack is enough to trigger a CoG action**.

The 'leaders' have given themselves the power to declare a State of Emergency and trigger a CoG action for virtually any cause, even the thought that another country **might** attack. (Recently, Korea has been constantly threatening to attack the US, conveniently providing the 'leaders' with an ever-present trigger for a Continuity of Government response.)

Other events that could frighten our 'leaders' into their bunkers could include, massive rioting and civil unrest, disease, nuclear events, natural events (like the Yellowstone Caldera exploding) and extra-terrestrial events such as asteroids, comets and {yes, even} alien invasions).

But something as simple as a large number of billionaires being threatened with massive financial losses could trigger the CoG activity. (Remember, most governments work for the wealthiest of the elites; whether you want to admit it or not.) If the stock market 'crashes' a State of Emergency will be declared and a free America will no longer exist.

Also remember that in America, we have an aging electrical infrastructure that is extremely fragile. Even now, parts of the nation are susceptible to 'rolling brownouts' during the summer.

Recent legislation is aimed at eliminating the coal-fired power plants that supply roughly thirty-three percent of our electrical power. Natural gas provides another thirty-three percent, and nuclear reactors provide only twenty percent of our electric needs.

Pulling the coal-fired power plants from the mix places a greater burden on the other power supplying components (and, no, solar and wind power will NOT make up the difference).

Hydropower and renewable energy (geothermal, solar, wind, etc.) only provide thirteen percent of our energy. Anyone who thinks we can shut down the carbon fuels power plants without causing a national disaster is living a fool's dream. The government is well aware of these statistics and the potential threats, yet they continue to push toward this end result.

Expecting nuclear and renewable energy to compensate for the loss of two-thirds of our Nation's energy power source will result in a national crisis that may very well result in the need to declare a "State of Emergency'.

It has been said that civilization is only nine meals from anarchy. How many of population have gone three days without food? Not very many.

Our 'leaders' are working furiously to further their special interests, which are generally directly opposed to the interests and needs of the citizens and the country.

With a two-party political system, the elected officials owe allegiance to the party rather than to the government or the citizens who 'elected' them into their life of luxury.

We have career politicians who grant themselves pay raises and outrageous perks, while exempting themselves from the more onerous legislation they pass.

The laws of the land apply to the commoners, not the elites. In most cases, the legislation explicitly provides exemptions for the 'leaders' and their friends.

While most Americans are struggling to make ends meet and almost thirty percent of the work force is unemployed (if you believe the advertised unemployment rate, you're being foolish...do the math {hint: ninety-seven million unemployed out of three hundred and thirty million does NOT equal a five percent unemployment rate. The 'leaders' are playing with numbers to keep the citizens appeased.}).

The politicians barrage the working people with emails and paper mail, and television messages begging for your hard-earned money. "Please send me ten dollars so I can win the election (and continue my life of luxury, while your child goes to school barefoot)."

I've worked for forty years and I've never been in a position where I could leave my current job for extended periods of time as I seek different employment while drawing a full salary, and with full knowledge and expectation that I will still have my old job if I don't get the new one. For Politicians, this is the norm.

How many of the current and recent Presidential candidates resigned their political positions to seek a different position? None.

Our political hacks are fermenting racial hatred. Every day, they do something to further divide 'we the people' into 'us' and 'them', and 'those', etc. The 'leaders' who could resolve racial and religious tensions choose to do otherwise. Instead, they stoke the flames of racial and religious discord, with the very apparent intent to cause a racial or religious war that will decimate the masses.

The Stock Market is just a tool to pull money away from the vanishing 'middle class' and putting it in the pockets of the wealthy. It is no longer a viable indicator of economic strength.

Only the wealthy and fund managers have the ability to be legitimate' players' in the stock market, which has become little more than a money laundering mechanism and a tool to drain money from the retirement funds of the commoners.

When one talks about Social Security, which most working Americans have paid into with every paycheck for their entire working life, politicians view Social Security as an 'entitlement' that can be raided to line their own pockets,

Social Security is a MANDATORY retirement investment made by hard-working American citizens over the course of their careers. The 'leaders' see it as a free grazing ground for their greed. Yes, Americans ARE entitled to Social Security, but it is NOT an entitlement. Nor is it a fund to be given freely to those who have never paid into it.

For many years now, everything the governments have done has been geared toward disenfranchising the common person. In fact, one prominent 2016 Presidential candidate proudly bragged while abroad, that the American government, '…taxes anything and everything, just because we can." Today, Americans pay more in taxes than they pay for all of their basic living expenses combined.

On another front, countries around the world are being besieged by massive hordes of invading barbarians that have no respect or regard for the laws of the host countries.

These barbarians rob and rape at will, while demanding that the host country acquiesce to demands that the host become more like the (horrible) country they just fled. (The question one has to ask is, "If the country you left was so horrible and oppressive, why do you want to set up the same legal and social system in your 'host' country?")

The 'leaders' of the host countries do nothing to stem the flow or punish or educate the refugees; even going so far as to 'protect' the barbarians from punishment or responsibility for their crimes.

In many countries, it is unacceptable or even illegal to criticize or complain about these invaders or their actions. Some countries even advise their citizens to change their lifestyles to accommodate the needs and desires of the barbarians.

While many of our veterans and poor are homeless and starving, the governments of the world continue to invite these mass invasions of barbaric cultures that challenge and threaten our way of life and civilization itself.

In most cases, the invading hordes are welcomed and protected and cared for while the host citizens suffer and die. This will ultimately result in civil unrest and a "State of Emergency'. It will actually become a revolutionary war as the citizens try to rid the world of the parasites.

Why are the governments doing this? Simply to set the stage for an event that they deem appropriate to invoke a CoG activity; including Martial Law, or more likely, a 'State of Emergency'.

Remember that the only ones who will benefit from the declaration of a 'State of Emergency' will be the 'elites' and the 'leaders'; all others will suffer horribly.

During a 'State of Emergency', the 'leaders' and other elites will have all of the privilege and benefits while the masses are forgotten and herded like cattle. The citizens will become enslaved labor and soldiers.

Hastening such a state will be extremely beneficial to the 'leaders', who can then continue to live their privileged lives without having to worry about the commoners. Once the commoners are devastated and marginalized, the power of the 'elites' will be absolute and irreversible.

Remember, EO 11051 (or its successor) mandates the activation of all Executive Orders in times of increased international tensions and economic or financial crisis.

This means that if there is a 'run on the banks', a stock market failure, or even if a foreign country starts talking about attacking America (or any other country), a 'State of Emergency' can be declared and your rights are destroyed. (In other words, the President can declare a 'State of Emergency' at any time, for any reason and America will be instantly transformed into a dictatorship.)

Martial Law (State of Emergency)

What is Martial Law? Wikipedia defines Martial Law as "the imposition of the highest-ranking military officer as the military governor or as the head of the government, thus removing all power from the previous executive, legislative, and judicial branches of government. It is usually imposed temporarily when the government or civilian authorities fail to function effectively (e.g., maintain order and security, or provide essential services)."

Obviously, our 'leaders' do not want to relinquish their power to the military; so, while many conspiracy theorists and alarmists will rant about the approaching declaration of Martial law, the chances of that being implemented is highly unlikely.

The more realistic CoG action will be the declaration of a 'State of Emergency', which can be anything the 'leaders' deem appropriate.

A 'State of Emergency' allows for imposition of ALL of the restrictions provided by Martial Law, without relinquishing power and authority to the military. This means that the people who caused the problems will remain in power and continue to pillage the country.

With increasing frequency, small 'State of Emergencies' are being declared. Though usually localized, they are part of a desensitization process. Ultimately, the common citizen will become so accustomed to the implementation of a 'State of

Emergency' (somewhere), they will accept it without question; expecting it to pass quickly, like the previous 'trial balloons'.

When a 'State of Emergency' is determine to have expired is entirely discretionary and could become a permanent feature of life. As long as the 'Leader' says the emergency still exists, it does exist.

Nothing in the Executive Orders mandates, indicates, or implies and expiration time for a 'State of Emergency'. Remember that under a 'State of Emergency' you have no rights, you have no possessions, and you have no family. You are merely property.

The President has repeatedly scoffed at the mention of imposing Martial law, because he knows that it will not happen. If necessary, he will declare a 'State of Emergency" and ensure that his lifestyle is not interrupted. Remember, if Martial law is imposed, the civilian 'leaders' may be tried in military tribunal and even executed for their crimes.

Let me rephrase that, the advantage of declaring a 'State of Emergency' over Martial Law is obvious; the current 'leaders' continue their lives of privilege and abuse of power without being constrained by the military, or the possibility of facing criminal prosecutions.

Many conspiracy theorists fear the implementation of Martial Law, but it could actually be a good thing. Many of the criminals currently in power could be arrested and brought up on charges before a military tribunal.

Remember that a 'State of Emergency' can be used as a pretext for suspending rights and freedoms legally guaranteed under a country's **Constitution** and essentially establish a dictatorship, until the dictator decides the 'State of Emergency' is over. (Remember that no government will freely relinquish any power it has granted itself. Similarly, no dictator will willingly step down.)

A declaration of a 'State of Emergency' is merely a mechanism to keep the common citizens out of the way of the elite 'leaders' as they escape to their bunkers.

Most people do not realize that in the event of a serious disaster or Extinction Level Event (ELE), most governments plan of action is to NOT warn the citizens because that knowledge "…might incite panic." (Maybe I'm a bit unreasonable, but if you know the world is ending, I want to

16

know as well, so I can spend my final moments with my loved ones.)

Not warning the citizens of impending disaster is extremely selfish and malicious and displays blatant disregard for the well-being of the citizens that the government 'leaders' are sworn to protect.

This is a violation of the trust the citizens legitimately have in their government. Failure to share vital survival-related information with the citizenry voids the social contract between the government and the citizens.

This means that the laws of the government are no longer viable or relevant and that the citizens become responsible for their own protection.

As an example, if you hire a security guard to protect your family, but he runs away at the first sign of trouble, he will be fired and possibly held criminally responsible for his dereliction of duty.

The same principle applies to governments, when they are derelict in their duties and responsibilities to the citizens, the government needs to be 'fired' and the 'leaders' need to be held accountable.

Martial Law or the civilian equivalent is not about maintaining law and order; it is all about controlling the masses for as long as possible to allow the 'leaders' to escape with as little discomfort or disruption as possible.

Remember that Continuity of Government is all about ensuring that the wealthy 'elites' and 'leaders' can continue their privileged lifestyles with as little discomfort as possible; it has nothing to do with protecting the country or the citizens.

Who Pays for CoG

Again, the concept of planning for Continuity of Government sounds like a wonderfully logical activity.

But if the situation is so bad that the 'leaders' have to run to a heavily shielded bunker, it is unlikely there will be much of a country or population to manage.

In that case, the CoG bunkers and plans are in existence merely to provide for the continued existence of the "leaders', the most worthless component of the human race. They will truly become the Morlocks of H.G. Wells' "The Time Machine".

But since all of this CoG effort and construction is primarily for the benefit of the elites and 'leaders', are the wealthy paying for all of the effort and constructions? No.

The taxpayer, the common man and woman toiling at sometimes thankless jobs to provide for their families are being unfairly taxed.

Every hard-working citizen who pays taxes is contributing to the continued existence of our elite 'leaders' at the expense of their own families. (Again, it has recently been exposed that Americans pay more in taxes than all other living expenses combined.)

Think about that for a moment, the citizens are being taxed into poverty to provide for the wealthy 'leaders'. There is nothing in the plans to provide for the citizens.

Even if the bunkers were large enough to provide for a majority of the population, the greed of the 'leaders' would ensure that only a miniscule portion of the 'common man' would be allowed to join the elites and survive. (They might realize that they would need plumbers and electricians and janitors.)

Let's face reality here; the elite 'leaders' have cleverly placed themselves in a position where the common man and woman pay for everything and only the 'leaders' and a select few benefit from that effort.

This is a case of 'survival of the least fit'. Unworthy parasites are sucking the life from humanity while destroying civilization.

When you are unable to afford to buy your child or spouse new clothes, remember that the money went towards building and maintaining a secure stronghold to be used by the 'leaders' in the event that they make such a mess of the world that they need to cower underground.

While you and yours will be suffering and dying, the 'leaders' will be safe and comfortable in their bunker; wining and dining and enjoying the good life.

If you doubt that you're paying for the extravagant lifestyles of our 'leaders' who will do everything possible to ensure their continued comfortable existence, then review the Government Budget.

There are countless 'redacted' line items and obscure programs no one can explain, 'for security reasons'.

Until recently, there were five or six years in succession that Congress failed to produce a constitutionally required annual budget. (If I failed to produce a required document at work, I would be fired; Congress gives themselves raises.)

Why do you imagine there was no budget for five years? It certainly was not a partisan matter because the Democrats and the Republicans each controlled Congress during some of those years. It was obviously a planned and coordinated activity; they wanted to spend as much as possible without the potential of ANY oversight.

Since they did finally provide an annual budget, it is a safe bet that their secret plans and construction are complete or nearing completion.

Additionally, countless billions of your tax dollars go overseas to support the United Nations and countries that 'hate' America. (I was taught to 'beat the stuffing' out of any bully that tried to take my lunch money.)

Our 'leaders' seem content to pay their bribes to the world; ensuring their own position in the elite hierarchy. Or perhaps they are ensuring that more of their parasitic kind will survive.

However, those billions of American taxpayer dollars sent as bribes to other countries is not reaching the citizens of those countries. Nor is all of that money going toward defense.

Much of that money disappears and is never accounted for. (I don't recall authorizing my government to tax me on behalf of a foreign government.)

A similar scheme is employed by International charities, where '…for just a dollar a day, you can feed and clothe and heal a child…" Typically, these scams are hosted by celebrities who can't be bothered with contributing to the charity. In fact, most of them are very likely paid handsomely for their services.

Obviously, the 'elites' know things the common citizen does not. They are withholding vital information from the citizens, in the interest of 'National Security'. ('National Security' is a code word for 'I want to always have the advantage'.)

Who does CoG protect?

The average person probably assumes that Continuity of Government implies the continued 'normal' operation of the government in such a manner that would have minimal impact of the daily lives of ordinary citizens. That assumption is completely incorrect.

CoG, by definition is designed to protect those responsible for the continued operation of our government. But just who does that include?

Are spouses and families of our elite 'leaders' included? Absolutely! (Unless the spouse and family of a specific 'leader' is deemed unsuitable…makes for a convenient way for a politician to get rid of an unwanted spouse.)

What branches of the government are among the 'chosen"? Is there a need for Congress or the Supreme Court if the Constitution has been suspended? Not likely.

Is there a need for Congress? No, but rest assured many of them have guaranteed themselves a seat in that bunker. (However, the Speaker of the house may be surprised to learn that he has to clean toilets for the real 'leaders' in order to retain his safe position and avoid being 'voted off the island'.)

What about the bureaucracies, like the IRS, Department of Justice, Education, Labor, Transportation, etc.?

It quickly becomes apparent that, from a realistic perspective, unless there are thousands of massive bunkers spread across the country, most of the rank and file bureaucrats will be tossed aside like so much garbage; only their 'masters' will have an opportunity to survive.

TSA and DHS and even the military will be used to distract and delay the enraged citizenry, and then summarily discarded.

TSA was instituted, not to protect the travel systems, but to methodically indoctrinate the citizens to 'follow orders' and obey; nothing more.

On the surface, the TSA is one of the most ineffective creations in the history of mankind. However, if you look closely, the one thing it does well is to herd humans around like animals, training them into obedience.

Always keep in mind that a Continuity of Government action or plan protects the Government and its highest officials. It has nothing to do with protecting the country or its citizens.

Bureaucrats at all levels are completely disposable. From the federal perspective, the state and local leadership is equally valueless.

Most governments have adopted the concept of planning for Continuity of Government (CoG). World War II and the Cold War were the driving impetus behind this movement.

Today, virtually every 'leader' and dictator has plans for Continuity of Government, which translates as 'Continuity of my power and privilege.'

While the planning and construction was in progress, the governments made no mention of these activities to the citizenry, lest they begin asking questions that might slow down progress.

Now, with most of the planning and construction complete, many governments now freely talk about Continuity of Government, as if it is a good thing. (I guess it could be considered a good thing, since it means all of the worthless talkers will be locked safely out of the way... we just need to lose the key to their bunkers so they can never again see the light of day.)

In actuality, Continuity of Government is a wonderful concept, IF you are part of the Government 'Elite'.

Remember CoG is designed to protect those in power so that they may ostensibly 'protect' you and yours; all while safely ensconced in a super-impregnable bunker with all of the luxuries readily available.

While the Government 'leaders' and their 'elite' companions wine and dine in the lap of luxury, safely protected from whatever fate they abandoned the citizenry to, the people who funded the CoG bunkers will be left to fend for themselves in a hostile world not of their making.

CoG is NOT designed to protect the vast majority of the population. Let me repeat that, <u>CoG is NOT designed to protect the vast majority of the population</u>. **The average taxpayer will never see any benefit from Continuity of Government planning or spending.**

While the 'leaders' may offer some token solution for the menace that drove them underground, human nature tells me that they will enjoy their safety and comforts, conveniently forgetting about the citizens. (Senator John F. Kennedy openly wept the first time he saw the slums of the Projects; he had been so insulated in his own privileged world that he had no idea that people actually lived in such dangerous squalor.)

The 'elites' are too far removed from reality to understand the suffering of the masses. Again, to most of them, the citizens are completely expendable,

Just remember that Continuity of Government is not intended to protect the citizens, it is designed to protect the 'elites'.

When a CoG event is over and it is 'safe', the 'leaders' will miraculously re-emerge from the bowels of the Earth to resume the leadership of the human race.

CoG Is Persistent

The CoG mentality cannot be removed. In every historical instance where an abusive government with a history of repeated injuries and usurpations, all having in direct object the establishment of an absolute tyranny over the general populace has been overthrown; it is not long before a new, equally abusive government rises to power. **Evil rushes in to fill the void left by its predecessor.**

In America, the colonies threw off the yoke of British rule, only to be replaced by an equally despotic government a few hundred years later.

In Russia, at the turn of the twentieth century, the Communists overthrew the Royal family and replaced them with an even more abusive form of government that collapsed form its own corruption less than a hundred years later; to be replaced by what is essentially a dictatorship.

In every revolution, the old government and 'leaders' are replaced by equally corrupt 'leaders' and governments. However, some of the old regime are often retained because, 'they know things'.

Anytime there is a void in 'leadership', someone equally unqualified to rule rushes in to fill that void; turning the engine of government into a tool to enrich them and theirs.

There is no recorded instance where an evil, corrupt regime was replaced by a long-lasting benign form of government. Government is an artificial and temporary construct, in spite of the fact that it constantly revives itself.

All governments and 'leaders' seek to perpetuate their power and control; typically at the expense of everyone else. That is fact. Humans appear to need to be ruled and dominated by others. This is a need that entirely too many politicians are willing to exploit.

If there is a revolution and the incumbent government is ousted and even executed, the new 'leaders', who probably railed against Continuity of Government plans, will suddenly determine that CoG is good and beneficial and that all previous plans should remain in effect and even improved upon.

Continuity of Government (CoG) is an evil, artificial construct that, once instituted, will never go away. It is the greatest deception ever imposed on any civilization.

Civilian CoG

But do not be deceived into thinking the CoG concepts are limited to governments. The wealthy 'elites' are well aware that they may not be invited into the sanctuaries of the incumbent 'leaders'. Many of them are building, or have built, their own sanctuaries. (They may be 'playing the odds' that the incumbent 'leaders' will perish and leave a void to rush into.)

While the taxpayer may not be directly funding these shelters, there is a strong likelihood that government funds are being diverted to allow the 'elites' to preserve their lifestyles without impacting their bank accounts.

While the average citizen is kept safely insulated from knowledge of any pending threat to their survival, the 'elites' are patently aware of the dangers before us.

There has been a recent surge of bunker construction by the wealthy. One has to ask, "What knowledge have they been given access to that the average citizen has been denied?"

Thousands of millionaires are fleeing the giant cities and many of them are building their private sanctuaries; it is to be assumed they expect to cower in their bunkers and 'weather' whatever crisis they have been warned about, presumably to protect them against the threat posed by the 'general public'.

My guess is that the wealthy are building shelters to protect them from the enraged masses of citizens who may finally rise up and regain control of their government and their lives. Most of the wealthy did not earn their wealth, it was given to them or they took it by force and deception.

From a more sinister perspective, the bunkers may be intended to protect the wealthy from biological or chemical agents soon to be released upon world's citizens by their governments in efforts to achieve a ninety-five percent reduction in the human population, preserving the world's one percenters with a token four percent to perform the manual, mundane, and dangerous functions necessary to keep the one percent living a life of luxury.

The concept of reducing the world's population by ninety-five percent has been presented in the "Apocalypse Equation",

"Apocalypse Theorem", "Apocalypse Theory" and other documents.

This population reduction philosophy is expressed on Georgia Guide Stones, which is a granite monument erected in 1980 in Elbert County, Georgia.

The first of the ten rules inscribed on the stones is "Maintain humanity under 500,000,000 in perpetual balance with nature". This indicates a desire to reduce the population to five to seven percent of existing levels; in other words, the annihilation of more than six and a half billion people worldwide.

When you look at what the 'leaders' have done to protect themselves and what the wealthy are currently doing along the same lines, you should have a very 'uneasy' feeling about your future.

If you haven't been informed about the bunkers, then you may be part of the ninety-five percent of the world's population that is deemed expendable and undesirable.

The 'elites' and the 'leaders' appear to have taken it upon themselves to determine who has the right to live and who should die. (Have you received your 'gold ticket' yet?)

Secret construction projects by the wealthy are nothing new. In the early twentieth century, the wealthy even built secret railroads, most notably under New York City.

Ostensibly, this was so they could avoid contact with the commoners. Reportedly, President Roosevelt used these railways to travel so he would not be exposed to the public too often in his disabled condition.

The degree of actual functionality and usage is largely undocumented and the rails are reportedly abandoned. (Of course, it is the government making these statements.)

However, the seed of an idea had been planted and there are rumors that there are sophisticated subterranean railways connecting major cities and strategic facilities, allowing the 'leaders' to travel in secret comfort without any record or observation. And this travel is executed all without the 'elites' being exposed to any hazards that might exist on the surface.

Whether this rumor is true or merely urban legend is open for conjecture. However, it might explain some of the strange noises people have been reporting across the country.

The point is that the 'elites' and the 'leaders' have long considered themselves above the masses and have taken great

24

pains to ensure that their travel is not inconvenienced by any unnecessary exposure to the common man and woman. They are the masters and we are their slaves.

State of Emergency

As mentioned earlier, a 'State of Emergency' can be declared at any time for virtually any reason, and when it happens, you have no rights, according to the 'leaders'.

There are constant rumors of secret FEMA concentration camps around the country. I have documented nearly a hundred of them in a separate, upcoming publication.

But if the truth be known, anything can become a concentration camp' a sports stadium, a shopping mall, even a school yard. When hurricane Sandy struck, FEMA set up a tent city where citizens were held hostage, without the freedom to depart, and with limited facilities.

Most countries, and especially America have a history of moving portions of its populations to concentration camps. The African-American slaves were held on the work camps known as plantations, the Native Americans have been conveniently moved to concentration camps called reservations. During World War II, the American-born Japanese were moved to desert concentration camps, forfeiting all of their possessions.

The Hispanics who have a history of invading America illegally have been deported. In the 1930s, there was the Mexican Repatriation Program to return 500,000 illegal immigrants. In 1954, Eisenhower instituted Operation Wetback, in which a million illegal immigrants were returned to their native country.

The American government has demonstrated that it has the ability and the willingness to impose its will on segments of the citizenry.

Over the past few years, I have had the opportunity to talk with a few high-ranking Marine Corp officers.

The first one mentioned that the armed forces have been training elite components of the respective branches to deal with civil unrest and how to contain vast numbers of the population.

In a different conversation, a second officer proudly boasted that they have been training for years and can easily turn a city of more than a million people into a prison camp overnight.

While FEMA may use platitudes about how they have the resources to take care of the people, their intentions are suspect.

Personally, I prefer to depend on my friends, family, and personal capabilities over those of some disinterested third party who is following someone else's orders and plans. I see no purpose in surrendering my freedom to some unknown, secretive organization that has suddenly decided it has total dominion over me and everything in my life.

Human nature cannot be trusted. This may sound paranoid, but history proves this statement. People will ALWAYS do what promotes their self-interests above those of others. If someone is in a position of power, they will do all that is necessary to retain and grow that power so that they may perpetuate their comfortable lifestyle.

CoG and You

Continuity of Government, in whatever form, is a part of everyone's life. It is a vile evil that touches everyone.

When (not if) a 'State of Emergency' is declared, the first general response will be surprise, followed by expectation of free 'stuff', followed by resentment and anger when events do not transpire as one expects, and finally mindless violence against anyone who happens to be available.

But what can the common citizen do about it? The way to deal with CoG efforts is to expect them to occur and be vigilant. Make your own plans for survival and independence. Do not be too willing to sacrifice your freedom for a brief period of security or comfort.

In the event that something horrible happens and a 'State of Emergency' is declared, tend to your friends and family. Be wary of local community organizers who want to have a committee to identify who has what skills and resources and how they should be shared. You may find that you are doing all of the giving and all of the work while someone else sits around and complains about how little they have.

Most dwellings are indefensible against even an unorganized mob. Make sure you have a safe place to go and 'ride out' any 'State of Emergency'. Never tell anyone what supplies you have, where you might plan to escape to, or what weapons you have.

Even at the local Home Owner's Association level (HOA), I have seen HOA board members declare that if something bad happens, they will go door to door to collect food, medicine, and weapons. My response was that they could have mine, one bullet at a time.

The ideal position to be in during a 'State of Emergency' is to be completely anonymous and invisible.

Epilog

Watch the 'leaders' and hear what they say and do not say. Many of them are so proud of their elite status that they tend to underestimate the intellect of their citizens.

Some of them will provide thinly-veiled hints about their plans. Be wary when they say things like, "The end of the republic has never looked better,"

If the 'leaders' and 'Political Class' and the 'elites' start to become unavailable, it may signal it's time to prepare yourself. Remember, most of these people are narcissists and require almost constant adoration from their slaves and fans. When they 'go 'out of pocket' for any length of time, or in large numbers, it could be a sign that something terrible is about to happen.

Again, the 'leaders' do not want the common people getting in the way of their pampered existence, so there will be little or no formal warning of a catastrophe.

As a citizen, you are expendable. If the government 'leaders' can comfortably contemplate and plan for the mass annihilation of billions of people to secure a 'better' life for themselves, it clearly demonstrates that you have absolutely no value. As such, you are completely expendable and can be freely disposed of at the whim of any government official.

You must depend upon your own wits and native intellect to determine risks and threats. Survival is your responsibility, not someone else's. Do not depend on the government to provide for you. If you do, you will die horribly.

Do not expect the President to stand before the camera and warn of an imminent threat until he is safely protected in his CoG bunker. He can't be bothered with helping or protecting the citizens.

Finally, if anyone in the government or any other political construct starts talking about Continuity of Government, this is a very bad sign. It could well mean that things are so bad that the 'upper class' is breaking ranks and some of them are 'going rogue'; probably because they just found out that their presumed spot in the bunker was given to someone else.

I would suspect that there will be high level accidents and assassinations immediately preceding a CoG event. It will be somewhat of a 'purge' of some of the more troublesome 'elites', or those who talk a bit too freely.

- Why does the government and the 'leaders' feel they need to make plans for controlling a vast percentage of the population?
- Why are there even discussions about reducing the population?
- Why is there a sudden 'concern' about global warming?
- Why has the government decided that virtually any activity is a 'sign of mental illness'?
- Why does the government feel it must act in secrecy in the interest of 'National Security'? (I have a pretty strong interest in 'National Security')
- Why are our tax dollars being sent overseas to support regimes that hate America?
- Why should a committee of despots (the UN) be given a voice in our national policies?
- Why does the government even have a 'black budget', with elements so secret that most of Congress is unable to review?
- Why do two 'parties' have a chokehold on American politics and government?
- Why have Americans surrendered their freedom and pride for a welfare check and a cell phone?

Wake up, America! Wake up, World! The citizens of planet Earth are being prodded and herded like cattle going to slaughter, and no one seems to see the signs.

###

Additional works by Ronald N. Goulden

http://www.rongoulden.com/Literary.htm

	The American Constitution
The American Constitution	https://www.createspace.com/4125797
The Apocalypse Theorem	The Apocalypse Theorem
	https://www.createspace.com/4173774
Survival II	Survival II
	https://www.createspace.com/4219712